Chi's
Sweet Adventures

②

Created by Konami Kanata
Adapted by Kinoko Natsume

VERTICAL COMICS

Chi's Sweet Adventures ②

contents

Chi Freezes, Part 1

IT'S A BLACKOUT!!

OH, DEAR.

MY DATA!

PCHK

HM?

THE TEMPER-ATURE IN THE ROOM IS SUDDENLY DROPPING!!

VWOOOOSH

BWWN

WAH!!

WASSAT? WHAT'S WRONG?

IT'S COLD!!

LET'S PUT ON COATS.

MYA?

Ftt

HUH?

30 min later...

IT'S COWLD.

Continued in Part 2

Chi Freezes, Part 2

4

Continued in Part 3

Chi Freezes, Part 3

*The phrase "cat tongued" refers to people who don't like hot food or drink.

Continued in Part 4

Chi Freezes, Part 4

Continued in Part 5

Chi Freezes, Part 5

        Continued in Part 6

Chi Freezes, Part 6

 CHI CAN'T FIND A SUN-BATHE OR A WARM COZY. TOTTR TOTTR

 IF YOU SLEEP THERE, YOU'LL CATCH A COLD!

 CHI CAN'T GO ON... FWOP

 I'LL GET A BLANKET FOR YOU.

 SWEEPY... SNOOO

 THERE WE GO!!

 OH, CHI?!

 IT'S WARM AND COZY. MMNNN

8

Continued in Part 7

The End

Chi Has Lessons Again, Part 1

Continued in Part 2

Chi Has Lessons Again, Part 2

11

Continued in Part 3

Chi Has Lessons Again, Part 3

12

Continued in Part 4

Chi Has Lessons Again, Part 4

13

Continued in Part 5

Chi Has Lessons Again, Part 5

Continued in Part 6

Chi Has Lessons Again, Part 6

Continued in Part 7

Chi Has Lessons Again, Part 7

The End

Chi is Scolded, Part 1

17

Continued in Part 2

Chi is Scolded, Part 2

CHI, GO PLAY OVER THERE.

SHNIK

IRK   IRK

WHAT...

IS THERE SOMETHING ELSE THAT'S FUN...?

OH...

HRRM.
CHOMP

CHOMP

MYAA!

OOH, SCWATCH SCWATCH! SCRATCH

THIS IS FUN!

SCRATCH

NOT THIS.

SMAK
SMAK

CHI, STOP THAT!!

MYA!

MOMMY, YOU WANNA SCWATCH SCWATCH, TOO?

SCRATCH   SCRATCH

Continued in Part 3

Continued in Part 4

20

Continued in Part 5

Chi is Scolded, Part 5

21

Continued in Part 6

Chi is Scolded, Part 6

22

Continued in Part 7

Chi is Scolded, Part 7

CHI'S BIT OF MISCHIEF

HELPED TO INSPIRE ME!!

OKAY! I'M GOING TO BRUSH YOU LOTS!

MYA!

ONLY A CAT COULD THINK

AS FREELY AS THAT.

OH, LOOKS LIKE YOU'RE HAVING FUN.

CHI HELPED ME, SO I'M THANKING HER.

THANKS, CHI!

PET PET

MYA?

AND SHE HELPED ME BY BEING GOOD DURING HER CLAW TRIMMING.

RIGHT?

DADDY, DO THE BWUSHY BWUSH MORE!

MYAAA!

A LOT HAPPENED,

CHI, YOU'RE A GOOD KITTY!!

BUT IT'S OK!

HAWAA!

The End

Chi Has Lessons Once More, Part 1

Continued in Part 2

Chi Has Lessons Once More, Part 2

LESSON 6

MRR. LESSON 6 IS "INVESTIGATE YOUR FOOD"~

BUT CHI'S SURE IT'S OK! SPARKLE SPARKLE

MYA...!

DON'T EAT ANYTHING EXCEPT SAFE PREY,

MRR MRR.

NO MATTER HOW HUNGRY YOU ARE.

TRY SNIFFING IT.

MRR.

WHY? IT'S BAD?

LOOK CLOSELY AT IT.

LESSEE...

SNIFF SNIFF

THE COLOR IS BAD, AND FLIES ARE GATHERING AROUND IT, SEE? IT'S ROTTEN.

...IT'S WOTTEN?

BLECH!!

MRAAOW!!

THERE YOU HAVE IT.

25

Continued in Part 3

Chi Has Lessons Once More, Part 3

MRGH.

LESSON 7 IS "MAKE SURE YOU HAVE A SAFE SPOT!"

LESSON 7

THE ROOFTOP IS WARM AND HAS A BETTER VANTAGE POINT.

YEAH, GOOD CHOICE!!

A SAFE SPOT?

Snake

Dog

IT'S A PLACE WHERE DANGEROUS THINGS CAN'T ENTER.

THEN LET'S TRY GOING.

MRGH.

HOP

IT'S HARD FOR THEM TO FIND YOU IN DARK AND SMALL PLACES LIKE THIS.

MYAAA!

CHI GETS IT!!

YAY! CHI'S GOING, TOO!!

MYAAA!

BUT IT'S A WITTLE COWLD.

YEAH.

MRAG!

SPLAT

OH, RIGHT, SHE STILL CAN'T JUMP...

26

Continued in Part 4

Chi Has Lessons Once More, Part 4

LET'S GO TO THE NEXT SPOT!

MYAN!

WAIT.

MRR.

YAY! THIS IS FUN!!

MYAAN!

MRGH.

BE CAREFUL NOT TO FALL AS YOU WALK.

WHEN YOU MOVE, MAKE SURE YOU WALK ON SAFE PLACES.

HUH?

RUFF RUFF!

~JOLT

MYA?!

THE WIDE ROADS CAN BE DANGEROUS.

VROON

PANT

PANT

AAH!!

CHI!!

MYAAA!!

SCURRY

SCURRY

WALK ALONG NOOKS AND PLACES NEAR WALLS LIKE THIS.

MYAA{

THE BARKY ONE IS SCAWY.

THAT DOG CAN'T GET ON THIS WALL, SO YOU DON'T HAVE TO RUN AWAY.

MRRM...

27

Continued in Part 5

Chi Has Lessons Once More, Part 5

28

Continued in Part 6

Chi Has Lessons Once More, Part 6

OKAY, LET'S TAKE SHELTER HERE.

ZHAAAA

MYAAA!

CHI'S NOT SLEEPY! THIS IS BORING!

...WHEW.

HAAA...

...

...

HEY, BLACKIE, WHAT SHOULD WE PWAY?

MYA?

BE PATIENT UNTIL THE RAIN STOPS.

MRR.

WAVER

RIGHT NOW, IT'S BEST TO SLEEP.

WHAT?

MRGH.

Continued in Part 7

Chi Has Lessons Once More, Part 7

One day later...

I'LL CHECK ON WHETHER THE LESSONS HAVE HAD RESULTS.

Y A A A W N

WAIN WON'T FALL.

IT'S NOT LIKE CHI WOULD REVIEW THEM... I WONDER IF SHE'S DOING ALL RIGHT.

MRR...

HOME WEALLY IS THE BEST.

Chi, it's your favorite pancakes!

MYAA~ ♡

THERE'S NO SMELLY PWEY,

...

CHI, LET'S PLAY!

MYAA!

THERE'S NO BARKY.

IT LOOKS LIKE SHE'S DOING JUST FINE.

The End

Chi Exercises, Part 1

Continued in Part 2

Chi Exercises, Part 2

I'M GONNA LOSE WEIGHT!

THEN

SWIP

CAN YOU DO THIS?!

MYAA.

MOMMY, WHAT'RE YOU DOING?

LATER, OKAY? MOM'S BUSY RIGHT NOW.

YAH!!

HUP...

HOW'S THAT?

MYA

THIS IS FUN!

UUGGH...

WIGGL

CH-CHI CAN'T DO IT~

MYA...

WIGGL

CHI'S GONNA DO IT, TOO!!

MYAA.

OH! WELL DONE!

I WON!!

?

32

Continued in Part 3

Chi Exercises, Part 3

The End

A Day in Blackie's Life, Part 1

WELL THEN, GUESS I'LL HEAD OUT SOON.

MRR.

MRGH...

THUMP   THUMP

RUSTL

Casual Oden

HERE YOU GO.

MEOW   MEOW

CHI'S HUNGWY.

MYAA.

Mraow!

CHI, HERE'S FOOD.

MYA!

YAY!

GOOD.

ALL IN ORDER!

MRR.

Continued in Part 2

Continued in Part 3

A Day in Blackie's Life, Part 3

Continued in Part 4

A Day in Blackie's Life, Part 4

37

Continued in Part 5

A Day in Blackie's Life, Part 5

38

Continued in Part 6

A Day in Blackie's Life, Part 6

COME TO THINK OF IT, THE LITTLE ONE ISN'T HERE...

MYA~

TIP

TIP

HMMM...

STAAAARE

HEY KID, WHAT ARE YOU DOING?

MYA?

NYAA

WHO WAS IT...

WHAT?

MYA~

I'M LOOKING FOR THE LITTLE ONE!

MYA~

NYA?

OH?

WHAT ARE YOU DOING?

MRGH.

OH, IT'S BLACKIE!

I'VE SEEN YOU BEFORE, HAVEN'T I?

MYA?!

LOOM

AUNTIE HERE SAID SHE KNOWS ME!

MYA!

MRR?

IS THAT SO?

MEW~

HMM...

39

Continued in Part 7

The End

Chi Gathers, Part 1

Continued in Part 2

Chi Gathers, Part 2

A GATHERING IS...

MRR.

DON'T RUN! DON'T MAKE A FUSS!

MRGHG!

BUT... SHE'S NOT LISTENING.

WHOAA?!

MYAA?!

MYAAA!!

SHEESH, I GUESS THIS KID IS STILL TOO YOUNG.

WHAT'S THIS?

THERE'S SO MANY!

MYAA!!

OH, IT'S THAT KID!!

MYA!

THIS IS THE GATHERING.

MRRM.

MYAAA!!

YAY!!

SCURRY

YOU CAME, TOO, LITTLE ONE?

MYAA

I'M NOT LITTLE! I'M COCCHI!

MRAR!

Continued in Part 3

Chi Gathers, Part 3

Continued in Part 4

Chi Gathers, Part 4

45

Continued in Part 5

Chi Gathers, Part 5

46

Continued in Part 6

Chi Gathers, Part 6

Continued in Part 7

Chi Gathers, Part 7

The End

I'M HEADED OUT!

ZAHA
RUSTL
RUSTL
ZAHAHA
RATTLE RATTLE
RATTLE RATTLE

YOHEY? MOMMY? WHERE ARE YOU GOING? ♪

EEK!!
MYA!!

CHI'S GONNA FOLLOW THEM~

EEK~!
MYAAAA~!!
SCAWY~!
SKEDADDLE

HUH?

HUH? WHERE IS THIS?
MYA....?
haa haa
PHARMACY

49

Continued in Part 2

Chi Takes Shelter, Part 2

50

Continued in Part 3

Chi Takes Shelter, Part 3

Continued in Part 4

Chi Takes Shelter, Part 4

Continued in Part 5

Continued in Part 6

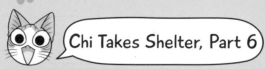

Chi Takes Shelter, Part 6

54

Continued in Part 7

Chi Takes Shelter, Part 7

55

The End

Chi is Worried Over, Part 1

THE RAIN STOPPED.

S P L A S H

WELL, I'M HEADED OFF.

WAH! CHI GOT DWENCHED!

OF COURSE YOU DID, YA DUMMY!!

...THAT WAS CLOSE...

EEK...

WHY DID YOU THINK WE TOOK SHELTER FROM THE RAIN?

CHI'S COMING, TOO.

SERIOUSLY, YOU'RE SO HELPLESS.

LIK
LIK
LIK

Continued in Part 2

Chi is Worried Over, Part 2

Continued in Part 3

Chi is Worried Over, Part 3

Continued in Part 4

Chi is Worried Over, Part 4

Continued in Part 5

Chi is Worried Over, Part 5

...?

HAAH.

WHOA ?!

URGH...

CHI THREW SOMETHING UP!

HURRY

WHAT, IT'S NOT A HAIRBALL?

HURRY

IT LOOKS LIKE MEAT!! SHE LOOKS ILL!

CHI DOESN'T FEEL GOOD...

KOFF KOFF

ANYWAY, LET'S GO TO THE VET!

MYAA~

LEGGO~

FLAIL FLAIL

BLECH

mii~

HURRY!

BRING HER VET ID!

60

Continued in Part 6

YAMANOTE VETERINARIAN

WELL, THERE'S NO NEED TO WORRY.

HISSSSS!

WHAT'RE YOU DOING!!

PCHK

LEGGO!!

HAAAAAH!

REALLY?

IT SEEMS TO BE FOOD POISONING FROM EATING SOMETHING OFF THE GROUND.

...

GOOD GIRL.

MYAAGH!

SHE VOMITED SEVERAL TIMES, SO LET'S GIVE HER AN IV.

CHI CAN'T STAND UP ANY-MORE.

MI...

REST FOR A WHILE.

FLUMP

GLINT

HUH?!

CHI IS SINKING...

SINKING...

SINKING DOWN...

61

Continued in Part 7

Chi is Worried Over, Part 7

CHI ...

SOMEONE IS CALLING...

OH, IT'S THE BEAR CAT... AND A RUNT CAT, TOO!

AH, SHE'S AWAKE.

YOHEY...?

BLINK

I WONDER IF THEY'RE CHI'S FRIENDS?

THEY MUST'VE COME BECAUSE THEY WERE WORRIED.

OH, SHE FELL BACK ASLEEP.

S N O O

EVERYONE'S HOPING CHI GETS WELL SOON.

SHE MUST BE SO TIRED.

CHI, GET BETTER SOON.

BUT CHI PROBABLY HAS NO IDEA.

The End

Chi Plays With Yohei, Part 1

63

Continued in Part 2

Chi Plays With Yohei, Part 2

64

Continued in Part 3

Chi Plays With Yohei, Part 3

HERE WE GO!

MYA!

YOHEI...!

S— SORRY...

HUP!

TOSS

TOSS

TOSS

MYAAA!

MYA?

BOING!

BOING

BOING!!

BOING

I SEE.

YOU WERE PLAYING TOGETHER.

OW 2!

AH!

MAKE SURE YOU CLEAN UP EVERYTHING.

WE'LL HAVE SNACKS AFTER.

YAY!

Continued in Part 4

Chi Plays With Yohei, Part 4

66

Continued in Part 5

Chi Plays With Yohei, Part 5

Continued in Part 6

Chi Plays With Yohei, Part 6

HAAH.

FWUMP

CHI IS STUFFED...

BUT I'M MORE GROWN UP THAN CHI IS!!

OH?

...IT'S SMALLER THAN THE LAST ONE.

THAT'S NOT TRUE.

A BIG BOY WOULD DO HIS PRACTICE DRILLS.

Math DRILL

URGH.

THEN MAYBE I'LL EAT IT!!

NOM

HRMM...

Math Drills

Big Boy

WHAT'S WRONG, YOHEY?

YUM!

GEEZ, YOU REALLY ARE A CHILD~

I'LL DO IT!! BECAUSE I'M A BIG BOY!

MYAA!

WE'RE PWAYING?! YAY!!

Continued in Part 7

Chi Plays With Yohei, Part 7

THIS IS BOWING...

MYAAU!

HEY, YOHEI! DINNER'S READY!

OH?

IS THERE SOMETHING

FUN TO DO?

WHAT IS IT?

SHH.

I'LL TRY SOMEWHERE ELSE.

OH, MY.

CHI?

YOU CAN NEVER TELL WHAT KIDS WILL DO.

69

The End

Chi Investigates, Part 1

70

Continued in Part 2

Chi Investigates, Part 2

Continued in Part 3

Chi Investigates, Part 3

I'M DETECTIVE SHERLOCK YOHEI HOLMES.

MYA?

OH, DID YOU FIND SOMETHING THAT FAST?

WASSAT?!

MYAA~!!

DASH

DR. WATSON! LET'S FIND THE FROG, FOR MOM'S SAKE!

YOHEY, WHAT IS IT?

STINKY.

MYAAN!

NO! THAT'S DAD'S SOCK!

DRAG

DRAG

DRAAAG

THE TRAIL GOES COLD RIGHT AROUND HERE.

...WHICH MEANS

MYAAA!!

WILL THIS NEXT THING BE A CLUE?!

THE CULPRIT IS HIDING IN THE WASHROOM!!

THIS IS FUN!!

MYA

NOT THAT!

BOING

BOING

72

Continued in Part 4

Chi Investigates, Part 4

Continued in Part 5

Chi Investigates, Part 5

Continued in Part 6

DR. WATSON, TAKE A LOOK AT THIS.

MYA MYA AAA!

SHRAK

SHRAK

THE CULPRIT LEFT A BODY DOUBLE BEHIND!

MYA MYA

DR. WATSON... CHI, THAT'S THE WRONG ONE!!

WASSAT?

MYAA~?!

...

haa

haa

SPLAT

HUH?!

AAA

NNG

...SOMETHING IS OFF...

75

Continued in Part 7

Chi Investigates, Part 7

The End

Chi Pals Around, Part 1

Continued in Part 2

Continued in Part 3

Continued in Part 4

Chi Pals Around, Part 4

Continued in Part 5

Continued in Part 6

Chi Pals Around, Part 6

Continued in Part 7

Chi Pals Around, Part 7

Continued in Part 8

 Continued in Part 9

Continued in Part 10

Chi Pals Around, Part 10

Continued in Part 11

Continued in Part 12

Chi Pals Around, Part 12

Continued in Part 13

HM? I TOOK MY EYES OFF THEM FOR A SECOND... WHERE'D THEY GO?

WHAT'S THIS? MRAR? RSTL

IT'S NOT LIKE I CARE... RSTL

YOU FOUND US~ MYA MYA! LET'S PLAY! SHFF MYAA!

...NOT HERE?

MRAR!!

WHERE ARE THEY? HM? RSTL RSTL

MYA MYA ~! MYAA! MRAARR!

Continued in Part 14

91

The End

FUKU FUKU

Kitten Tales

Konami Kanata

Craving More Cute Cat Comics?

Want to see more furry feline antics? A new series by Konami Kanata, author of the beloved *Chi's Sweet Home* series, tells the story of a tiny kitten named FukuFuku who lives with a kindly old lady. Each day brings something new to learn, the change of the seasons leads to exciting discoveries and even new objects to shred with freshly-grown claws.

Join FukuFuku and her charming owner on this quietly heartwarming journey of kittenhood.

Both Parts 1 and 2 On Sale Now!

Chi's Sweet

Coloring Book

Chi returns to the US in a coloring book featuring dozens of cute and furry illustrations from award-winning cartoonist Konami Kanata.

On Sale Now!

Chi's Sweet Adventures 2

Translation - Jan Cash
Production - Grace Lu
            Anthony Quintessenza

Translation provided by Vertical Comics, 2018
Published by Vertical Comics, an imprint of Vertical, Inc., New York

Originally published in Japanese as *Kyou no Koneko no Chi 2* by Kodansha, Ltd., 2017

This is a work of fiction.

ISBN: 978-1-947194-11-3

Manufactured in Canada

First Edition

Vertical, Inc.
451 Park Avenue South, 7th Floor
New York, NY 10016
www.vertical-comics.com

Vertical books are distributed through Penguin-Random House Publisher Services.